# Poems To Be Still By

Gloria —
Thank you so — I hope
you enjoy also!
                    Sincerely
                    Nora

# Poems To Be Still By

Nora Stilwell Jelley

**To order additional copies of this book, contact:**
Xlibris Corporation
1-888-795-4274
www.Xlibris.com
Orders@Xlibris.com
58134

# Contents

This collection of poems is dedicated to my daughters, Donna and Sharon, who are each a gift.

# Preface

In January 1887, Arlinda M.C.Veeder wrote a poem expressing her love for her daughter Jane, my grandmother. Her words portray so exactly my feelings for my daughters that I included it in this preface.

> Though cruel fate should bid us part
> As far's the pole and line;
> Her dear idea round my heart
> Should tenderly entwine.
>
> Tho' mountains frown and deserts howl
> and oceans roar between,
> yet, dearer than my deathless soul
> I still would love my Jane.
> Your Mother                    Linnie M.C. Veeder

Along this lineage came not only a love of poetry, but a love of stillness, a desire of God's heart in Psalm 46:10. It is my hope the reader will seek God's stillness.

# *For Jesse*

Lord, in the season of your birthday,
I want to thank you for the birthday of a precious grandson.
For his bright, delightful, rippling laughter
and for the gift of letting me hear it.
For the bubbling personality that lifts
my spirits and is like a burst of consuming sunshine.

A sunshine that warms my soul as intensely
as the actual sunbeams warm my skin.
When I contemplate how I love this grandson,
I realize how much you love me.

You loved me enough to give your precious Son
and my willful, obstinate spirit is broken with love.

And through the breaking,
comes strength and peace.

NSJelley

# Angels Among Us

There are angels among us,
Tho we cannot see where.
But our loving heavenly Father
has provided them with care.
The Bible speaks of angels,
in both Testaments, New and Old,
and they're one more gift
the Father gives us,
as in the Bible told.
So if you are aided by an angel
or feel there is one near,
give the praise to your heavenly Father,
He's the one who put them there.

NSJelley

# Pleasant Distraction

She had only cleaning on her mind
for she was one of the "organized kind."
Maintaining order of memories laid aside
when her eyes fell upon the stack of letters neatly tied.

Tied with a ribbon of days that are no more,
tied as the memories that in her heart were stored.
Like turning a key in an once locked door,
she opened the package bound up so secure.

She settled down like a cat in the sun,
all thoughts now gone of just "getting done."
The tenderness grew as she relived and refelt
and thought of the many things the passing years had dealt.

Words written in the present
that quickly became the past.
Words that formed her hopes and dreams
of the times that were to last.

A voice brought her back to reality,
then the knock upon the door
and she quickly tied the package
of the letters on the floor.

But the feeling would stay with her
a warm and steady glow
and she thanked her Heavenly Father
for the boy who loved her so.

NSJelley

# Have You Told The Children?

Have you told the children how this land
was fought and died for?
How at Bunker Hill the young men and the farmers
fought with pride?

It's important that they know
that our history really lived,
and young and old have battled side by side.

It's been struggled for
on foreign fields
from France to Corregidor,
by those whose names we'll never even know.
Skirmishes have been won and lost,
could anyone ever count the cost?

The seeds of pride in a beautiful land
Where God has blessed on every hand,
and men still seek His will and plan.
This too must be carefully taught.

In God's Holy Word, the Scriptures,
this verse we deeply cherish,
"Where there is no vision, the people perish."

NSJelley

# Between Friends

She serves me love in a cup of tea
and I know each day she prays for me.
It's not very often one gets a friend
who listens and cares and often mends.
Her anytime remedy is hot tea and spice
in a pretty cup, to make it real nice.

The spice is her humor-unique and rare,
it gives the tea flavor, no one could compare.
She listens me out of many dark moods
and love of the Lord she always includes.
She's really a gift God gave to me
and she serves me love in a cup of tea.

NSJelley

# Evelyn's Gift

On a lovely Christmas night
a sweet young girl of Swedish descent
brought cookies to the Christ Child,
to her, an exciting event.
She wore a crown of candles and ivy,
brought her gift on a silver tray,
but the life that lay before her
was the real gift for Him that day.

Her love for her Savior has
carried her through each and every day,
For she'd rather be His servant
than any other way.

Her choices and her conduct
have always been the "glue"
that kept her faithful on many a job
that no one else would do.

She'd be the first to tell you,
she's been covered by His grace,
covered with love in great measure
has always been the case.

Her sense of humor has carried her
through many a difficult time,
and her delight in others,
has kept that twinkle in her eyes.

So here before her family,
which really includes us all,
we take a moment to give Him praise,
for His faithfulness in all that she does.

NSJelley

# Four Questions From The Lord

A hurried prayer in a busy day,
"Where were you at our quiet time today?"

A muttered curse overheard on the job,
"When do you mention Me in praise?"

A hopelessness in the eyes of a neighbor,
"When will you tell them of Me?"

"Can you forgive me, Lord?",
my heart cries out,

"Of course," comes the answer in a question,
"Don't I love you?"

NSJelley

# Heavenly Motive

Can the skillful artist capture
the exact blue of the summer sky?
Can he create the gentleness
of a breeze that happens by?
The warmth of the sun in an open field,
keeps the tiny butterflies busy,
for every blossom feels so needed
that they keep the bees in a tizzy.

Oh, that we could capture
this perfect summer day,
and pull it out when all the world
is dusted with dismal gray.

But God in His great wisdom knew,
we needed contrast in our lives,
and as He gives us sunshine and rain,
He gives us also joy and some pain.

But his motive for all of these,
comes from above,
His motive always, always is love.

NSJelley

# His Way

The air I breathe,
the clothes I wear,
the food I eat,
the people I meet,
are all ordered from the Lord.

His mercies, new every morning,
May I never take for granted.
A contrite heart, I need to renew,
to cultivate the good He has planted.

To overcome sin, each and every day
with His strength, it's my wish to say,
today, I will do it His way.

NSJelley

# In Concert

Young man with a guitar,
you let God speak through your fingers
on the strings,
and say things to hearts opened by the Holy Spirit.
As your fingers fly, I begin to comprehend a new language.
The music speaks to my heart and
when the last chords stills and reality returns,
I am sure of this message.
I have heard God's love, so pure and inspired,
and I know I have heard more notes
than were played.

NSJelley

# Motives

Motives for actions,
Motives for views,
Are they quite simple,
or do they have the hues?

Are they base and selfish,
still bound by Satan's snare?
Or have they had the Master's touch,
compelled by love and care?

Lord, make my motives as the snowflakes
clean and pure, designed by Thee,
so that when the motives increase,
all will see the Christ in me.

As the snowfall covers fully,
so would all my life be filled
For it takes the skill of Jesus
showing me the Father's will.

NSJelley

# My Bible

A love letter is a personal thing,
very special, very precious, very dear.
And by far the best letter I've ever received
was written for all men to hear.

It covers a time span immortal to men
yet answers the questions of "now".
For the author is God, the Lord of us all,
for whom one day, each knee shall bow.

He wrote this letter
with pens of chosen few
and made it a masterpiece,
inspired for me and you.

Every book and every promise,
pictures Christ, His only Son, therein.
For it is belief in Jesus Christ
that saves us all from sin.

NSJelley

# My Gift

There's nothing like your first-born child,
a gift that changes your world.
Suddenly, dramatically, everything becomes new,
and your very reasons for living begin to come into view.

The years race by and you watch as she grows,
and she learns the tough lessons
that life often throws.
Her independence and joy
are her trademark to all,
(just don't push her too far,
she can be a brick wall!)
Then one day you realize your blessings have increased
and the very wonders of your gift
have never, ever ceased!

NSJelley

# Not So Trivial

It seems so small to say "thank you",
for Salvation, provision and health.
For mercy and guidance,
for care and direction,
a reason for life and its wealth.

But I bow before Him and praise Him,
and thank Him from deep in my heart,
a sinner now justified,
by His name glorified,
all because
He paid the ultimate price.

NSJelley

# One Step back

Very early in my life, I accepted God's gift.
His grace and His love were so real.
But as time went on, I wandered away,
away to the misty flats.
My soul was in pain, I hit an all-time low,
how I longed for the touch of His peace.
Then I found to my wonder, although I'd gone so far,
it took just one step back.

Just one step back to Calvary,
just one step back to the cross.
There I found His loving arms
encircled my heart,
and all the pain was a thing of the past.
I don't know why I struggled such a very long time,
struggled with shame and with guilt.
For the answer, His answer, was there all the time,
it was when I took one step back.

NSJelley

# Perspective

The child who strays,
thinks his parent is lost.
And many of us like children, are similarly so.
The Lord we seek
is really seeking us,
for He cares for "Whosover" will.

NSJelley

# Perhaps Today

I see the light of heaven
     breaking through the trees,
Is this the day my Lord will choose to come?

I feel His hand that guides me
     through my troubles dark and dense,
Is this the day my Lord will choose to come?

He left the Holy Spirit,
     to comfort and bring peace,
and when I seek to know His presence,
     His mercy does not cease.

So each and every day I wake
     I feel a special joy,
For this may be the very day,
     The Lord will choose to come!

NSJelley

# Prayer For A New Friend

Dear Lord,
I met a new found friend today
You put her in my way.
And tho we had not long to talk,
her heart had much to stay.

She said she loved you too, dear Lord,
praise God, we do agree,
but sadness filled her heart and eyes
I could not fail to see.

She said that they had lost a son,
and tho my heart reached out,
only one who has lost a child
could fully feel, no doubt.

"Sow in tears, reap in joy"
is the promise that God makes.
You see, pain was not a stranger
when Christ died for all men's sake.

But time will come when death is gone,
and tears will be no more.
And this dear heart will smile once more,
for Your love is the cure.

NSJelley

# Precious Helplessness

When we can do nothing whatever,
when we have no solution at all,
When we've tried every path of our own choice,
then with the "whole heart" on Jesus we'll call.

For it's helplessness that's the real key,
surrender of rebellion and will.
Recognition that God is in control
and can make the stormy heart still.
"We know not now, but we shall know"
Precious promise that He gave
and never will promise be broken,
He who gave it has conquered the grave.

This same Jesus of Nazareth
added His power to our helplessness,
And according to His own mercy and grace
attends to my heart's distress.

NSJelley

# Related Love

I have heard God's love described
as deeper than the sea,
but I find that I relate,
by what it means to me.

The laughter of a tiny child,
a tall and stately tree,
the tenderness of someone's eyes,
in gentle sympathy.

And if I were to doubt these things,
I've but to read again,
how God gave up His precious Son,
to suffer for my sin.

He died that I might never die,
but live with Him someday,
tho' I have not the slimmest hope,
this debt I could repay.

NSJelley

# Shut the Door, Gently

Shut the door gently, dear one, on your grief.
The one who has passed would not have you suffer,
suffer for an unending time.
Look to the Lord for the help He can give,
and boldly go on with life's tasks.
There is no betrayal in continuing on,
only honor and tribute to the one who has gone.
So shut the door oh so gently, and
carry, carry on.

NsJelley

# Stars In The Night

If you're wondering why God allows darkness,
and at times you can't see very far.
Remember that it's in the darkness,
when you look up, you see all the stars.

Looking up is the key to the problem,
you'll find the answers on high.
God promises a plan for the future,
and in time will explain reasons why.

So keep looking in an upward direction.
Have faith in each promise God makes.
God has loved you from the very beginning,
He gave His dear Son for your sake.

NSJelley

# Suffering

It comes sometimes in the dark of the night,
sometimes in a pristine setting,
this fear that draws our heartstrings so tight,
it threatens the very breath we are taking.
But Jesus is there, in the dark of the night,
He know about the fear.
His comfort and presence is always there,
for His suffering surpassed any other.
How shall we handle it,
this suffering, this fear?
His example, our only solution.
Courage in His name, dear child of the King,
So whatever the plan,
surrender to what God has planned.
Knowing and remembering each step of the way,
that His love remains in command.
Yes, courage, dear one,
for you are the child of a King!
whatever your plan,
remember, God is in control!

NSJelley

# Sugar & Spice

To look into the shining eyes
of a precious little girl,
is to look into the future
and see a better world

To see her grow and thrive on care,
lifts the weight of burdens we bear.

And when her laughter comes to mind,
we breathe a prayer for all mankind.

A prayer she'll learn the right from wrong,
and raise our lagging spirit's song.

Yes, the presence of this little girl,
like every little child,
is the song we need to guide our hearts,
and the hope to carry on.

NSJelley

# The Revelation

When Jesus died,
the woman cried,
the men were depressed and upset.
The Revelation of His own dear self,
had not happened yet.
Behold, what joy and thrill of soul,
when lo, the truth was known!
The Son of God, in Omniscient power,
had broken the seal of the tomb.
Seal of sin,
Seal of death now broken.
When Christ came forth
for you and me,
the Voice of God has spoken.

NSJelley

# The Way Back

Father, sometimes I feel that you've forgotten me.
Sometimes it seems that you don't care.
But Father, I suddenly realize that it's not you that doesn't care,
that I'm the one who hasn't loved and cared.

I haven't read your Word,
I haven't praised your Name,
I haven't even told you all the things that bother me.

So Father, I come now.
And humbly do repent
For I haven't even thanked you
for the precious Son you sent.

Lord, help me learn this
lesson well today.
Feelings aren't always "truth".
Your word is the only Way.

NSJelley

# Witnesses

I was witness to some special things today.
Each a touch of love in a slightly different way.
A Christian brother's encouragement
to a man who was feeling low.
A sisterly hug to someone
who really needed it so.
A young boy's smile at a teacher's attention,
small things for sure,
but worthy of mention.

Small things in our eyes,
but remember His Word.
His ways are not our ways,
by His love, our hearts are stirred.

NSJelley

# Uncharted Waters

Where is my ship going?
Through troubled waters?
Through sudden squalls?

But God has promised
come what may,
He'll be my captain all the way.

He'll still the wind and waves of life
and steer me through the times of strife.

He'll be my light through the blackest night,
He'll be my compass, showing wrong from right.

And when I land on that heavenly shore,
and my ship is about to moor,
one fact above all will ring out true,
'Twill be my Captain that brought me through!

NSJelley

# View Point

If I could look with a microscope
upon this hectic life,
and I could see as God does see,
what men would strive to be,
would I laugh with scorn and hate,
feel contempt for what was viewed?
Or would I feel compassion
for the futile things they do?

My view, that strains to stay aloft,
feels the gravity so strong,
and comprehension slips my grasp,
like the "mercury" of right and wrong.

Aware, so aware of my mortality,
I see my Great God's gift,
to give his Son, to drink the cup
to cause an eternal rift.

But greater love hath no man ever
this Son of man and God
who bridged the chasm just for us
a love no one can sever.

Tho' He'd given me my free will's choice
He relentlessly pursued
until His truth invaded my heart,
and grace and peace ensued.

He gathered me close in His sweet arms,
and I knew my life was complete__
and from that point on,
my greatest joy,
would be at the Master's feet.

NSJelley

# You First Loved Me

Lord,
You were broken,
that I might be mended.
You were weakened
that I might be strong.
You came in love,
that I might learn right from wrong.

Broken, weakened, crucified for me.
Not because I loved you,
but because you first loved me.

You came from heaven
that I might live abundantly.
You were made flesh
to dwell here among us.
To teach us to live in the world,
but not to be of the world.

Broken, weakened, crucified
for me.
Not because I loved you,
but because you first loved me.

You gave your life that I might be with you,
You took the Law
and conquered it with grace.
You did all this that I might meet you,
face to face.

Broken, weakened, crucified for me.
Not because I loved you,
but because you first loved me.

NSJelley

# Emily

I wish I could have known her
when she was a very young child.
I would have made her feel secure
and know she was worthwhile.

A photo shows this pretty child,
with dark and bouncy curls
that crowned her head and framed
her face with lovely wavey swirls.

But the photo can not tell us
that she never knew her mother
that she was raised by first one aunt,
then passed on to another.

But life is truly stranger than fiction,
and she is a living example
of one who was raised on a minimum love,
but when giving, she always has ample.

She wears her heart upon her sleeve
where its taken many a blow,
but it's too big to fit inside,
as many people know.

God gave her eyes a very special blue,
in a large field of larkspur,
you might match their hue.

And if their color had a sound,
it would be that of her laughter,
so delightful to one's ear,
that it stays in the heart long after.

Continued

Not always easy has been the way
of this small child of yesterday,
but courage is buried deep in her soul.

It's become an accepted part of her role
of wife and mother, of grandmother and friend.
All part of a special wonderful blend.

Some good, and some bad,
some rich and some poor,
the world has many a mother.
But I tell you from the depth of my soul,
I love her as no other

NSJelley

# Big Brother Bill

When I first met "Big Brother Bill",
I was filled with a sense of awe,
for was he not the oldest one,
and my title was "in-law"?

At family gatherings, the others voiced their views,
and on their words, he seemed to muse.
He seemed to have his own clear thoughts,
and knew which facts to use.
And when the timing was just right,
he'd share his thought-out perspective.
And others there would see the wisdom,
which til' then was out of sight.

In the years that have transpired,
I've learned his strength was not his own,
that the wisdom that often showed,
was really his "on loan".
God was his constant friend and mentor,
and led his every step,
and never failed when claim was made,
each promise made, was kept.

NSJelley

# Growth

The Lord gave me a young new plant
to care for day by day.
I keenly watched but couldn't see
a change in any way.

But then a few new leaves appeared,
and very soon a flower.
It was as if to prove a point
of God's abundant power.

God's Word says each one has a gift
and so, whatever mine,
it's rate of growth and time to bloom,
be "not my will, but Thine."

NSJelley

# Working Woman

She starts each new day with hopes and plans,
and counts each moment a treasure,
for they're given just once
and she strives to live them all
to their very fullest measure.

She sees the future,
as open and spacious,
with an eagerness of spirit
that's clear and vivacious.

Her memories have been sorted
so only the precious remain,
memories by which her soul will sustain.
They're stored away with some very special cares
and God is the only one with whom she shares.

But the charm of today
leaves no time for delay,
and much to do before sleep.
A new place to go, a chapter to read
a list never ending, a need.

She's learned it's the journey
that's the joy,
she knows the time to be happy is now.
to count her blessings each day,
than to put off 'till the "someday when".

NSJelley

# *Sondra*

She's my sister-in-law,
she's my sister-in-Christ,
she's one who's become very dear.
And all that she does, whatever she does,
she does with a heart that's sincere.

With a piece of color and dashes of know-how
and a keen sense of where a need is,
she pitches right into get the job done,
no matter how big the deed is.

She's been a sweet blessing
and meant a lot to me.
Her life's a "gentle testament"
of what Christ's love should be.

NSJelley

# Communion

It was Communion Sunday and as the Pastor spoke
and broke the bread and served the wine,
the Holy Spirit spoke to my heart and took my soul
into the universe.

He showed me worlds of uncharted space,
of which God was Creator and Ruler.
The magnitude
of earth's population and it's problems
were shown to me until my limited comprehension
was saturated and I was overwhelmed by it all.

I was alone with God and all else was gone.
But no, not alone for I held Jesus by the hand and I was not afraid.
I felt instead happiness and security, just being with Jesus.
For it was then I noticed the white warmth of His robe was wrapped
around me, securing me, protecting me.

I realized that this was Communion-remembrance,
that Jesus left all of this to suffer agony, separation
and finally, death, to be with me now.
He chose me that I might be with Him and know what
Love was all about.

NSJelley

# God's Choice

Without wings, birds could not fly,
without water, all fish would die,
and if you weren't part of my world everyday,
there'd be no reason for work or play.

You're the sunshine of my darkest hour,
you're life and breath and health,
and the richest one on this whole wide earth,
could never match my wealth.

Don't know what I've done to deserve you,
you're my gift of God's good grace.
But all the struggles are nothing,
when I look into your face.

I know whatever the problem
I know whatever the test,
God gave me a special partner,
to love and serve Him the best.

NSJelley

# Rebellion

An irritation. An abrasion. A roughness in the soul,
that even when my lips are silent,
stings and aches.
My steps are headed for the misty flats, and my eyes
strain and search.

I cannot see clearly because
things are blurry and undefined and fear creeps in
of that which I cannot see.

And then, almost mystically, I become aware of
warmth and light.
I see a breakthrough and indecision is no problem,
for I yearn for that Light.

There can be no mistake,
for that Light is "the Way, the Truth and the Life."
And suddenly, I am safe.

NSJelley

# *Spring*

It's been a winter plagued by illness,
it's been a season of cough syrup and pills,
but now hopefully the worst is over,
and I see it was all in His will.

For it was a time we were forced to seek Him,
a time His faithfulness was clear,
for when our need is greatest,
we find He is most near.

And with spring comes a time of renewal,
when the words of the Psalmist ring true.
"Restore to me the joy of Thy salvation!"
God's promises again proven true!

NSJelley

# Images

When I pictured my life as a garment,
it was not in a very good state.
It was torn and ragged and miserably worn,
edges frayed at an alarming rate.

But then the Christ of Gethsemane
showed me my image so clear
my sincere efforts were hopeless and vain,
but He said, "Leave your old garments here."

"I've purchased for you a brand new one.
The price has been paid and it's free.
My blood has been shed for this new one,
Only surrender is needed of thee."

So I yielded my old life to Jesus,
gave up what I really could not hold.
Then He puts His strong arms around me,
and welcomed me into the fold.

NSJelley

# Words

It's not the pain received that you remember,
not the tactless words at your expense.
When the years have passed on by,
you'll look back, perhaps to cry
at the thoughtless things and careless words
you spoke.

So be careful with your words
the world is listening to each one.
Remember, words could win a soul
for Jesus' sake.

So prayerfully consider
before you blurt them out,
for God should have control
of every one.

NSJelley

# A New Day

God's work is not always easy.
our path is not always smooth.
For sinful habits often form in us,
like potholes in the road.

But today is the day for beginnings.
New roads for Jesus need work,
and no inconvenience should hamper
no detail of His should we shirk.

NSJelley

# *Clarity*

When in my quiet time,
I make the choice to turn and boldly ask for
clarity.
God reveals to my often jumbled thoughts,
clarity.
And when I question and become argumentative,
I read His Word again, and I find
clarity
I can take no credit or applause
for grasping a truth within,
for He alone gives truth and sight,
and to my soul brings
clarity.

NSJelley

# Christmas Detour

The Scriptures tell of Wisemen
leaving home and country behind.
Fervently seeking the Christ Child,
King of the Jews, they would find.

Most wicked of men, King Herod,
did what he could to prevent.
But God had ordained and decreed
His star lead them to the One sent.

Worship and gifts of great value
were given on bended knee,
for finding and meeting the young Child,
fulfilled the great prophecy.

Evil was Herod's intention,
the Scriptures go on to say,
but by God's divine intervention
they traveled home a new way.

Wondrous story, down through the ages
of the Christ, Prince of Peace, Counselor,
tells how their lives were protected
as God changed their path evermore.

God's story is not finished,
for whosoever will may come.
They who seek, still can find,
be they sick, lame or blind
when they find Him, lives will be changed.

The message of Christmas is still here,
if we do as the Scriptures say.
And we worship and give Him the
gift of our heart, we too, will travel a different way.